Pennie Stoyles

The A–Z of
Health

Volume 3 F–J

Smart Apple Media
P.O. Box 3263
Mankato, MN, 56002

First published in 2010 by
MACMILLAN EDUCATION AUSTRALIA PTY LTD
15–19 Claremont St, South Yarra, Australia 3141

Visit our web site at www.macmillan.com.au or go directly to www.macmillanlibrary.com.au

Associated companies and representatives throughout the world.

Copyright © Pennie Stoyles 2010

Library of Congress Cataloging-in-Publication Data

Stoyles, Pennie.
    The A-Z of health / Pennie Stoyles.
        p. cm.
    Includes index.
    ISBN 978-1-59920-541-0 (library binding)
    ISBN 978-1-59920-542-7 (library binding)
    ISBN 978-1-59920-543-4 (library binding)
    ISBN 978-1-59920-544-1 (library binding)
    ISBN 978-1-59920-545-8 (library binding)
    ISBN 978-1-59920-546-5 (library binding)
    1. Medicine, Popular—Encyclopedias, Juvenile. 2. Health—Encyclopedias, Juvenile. I. Title.
    RC81.A2S76 2011
616.003--dc22

                                                                    2009038467

Edited by Julia Carlomagno and Gill Owens
Text and cover design by Ivan Finnegan, iF Design
Page layout by Raul Diche
Photo research by Legend Images
Illustrations by Andy Craig and Nives Porcellato, except for p. 12 (Guy Holt) and p. 30 (Alan Laver, Shelly
Communications)

Manufactured in China by Macmillan Production (Asia) Ltd.
Kwun Tong, Kowloon, Hong Kong
Supplier Code: CP December 2009

Acknowledgments
The author and the publisher are grateful to the following for permission to reproduce copyright material:

Front cover photo of a mother checking daughter's fever (or temperature), courtesy Jamie Grill/Getty
Images

Photographs courtesy of:
Bananastock, **11**; Comstock Images, **7** (cauliflower); © Stewart Cohen/Blend Images/Corbis, **31**; Corbis RF,
9; ERproductions Ltd/Getty Images, **8**; Adrian T Sumner/Getty Images, **26**; Art Vandalay/Getty Images,
18; © 2008 Jupiterimages Corporation, **10**, **19** (both); MACMILLAN\Haddon Davies, **7** (eggs); PHIL/CDC/
James Gathany, **28**; PHIL/CDC/Janice Haney Carr, **22**; Photolibrary © Bubbles Photolibrary/Alamy, **15**;
Photolibrary/Biology Media, **20**; Photolibrary/Scott Camazine, **29**; Photolibrary/Jose Luis Pelaez Inc, **25**;
Photolibrary/NIBSC/SPL, **24**; © Joseph Dilag/Shutterstock, **23**; © Sergey Peterman/Shutterstock, **6**;
© Jamie Wilson/Shutterstock, **5**.

While every care has been taken to trace and acknowledge copyright, the publisher tenders their apologies
for any accidental infringement where copyright has proved untraceable. Where the attempt has been
unsuccessful, the publisher welcomes information that would redress the situation.

Health

Welcome to the exciting world of health.

The A–Z of Health is about the healthy functioning of the body and mind. Health can mean:

- physical and mental health, including different body processes
- diseases and illnesses that affect health and well-being
- drugs, treatments, and ways to stay healthy

Volume 3 F–J   Health

They Said It!

"If you have health, you probably will be happy, and if you have health and happiness, you have all the wealth you need."

Elbert Hubbard, American philosopher

Fever is a rise in body temperature that is usually caused by an infection.

Rises in Body Temperature

Most people have a normal body temperature of about 98.6 degrees Fahrenheit (37 degrees Celsius), although this temperature may be slightly higher or lower in different people. If a person has an infection, he or she might develop a mild fever, in which body temperature rises to about 102°F (39°C). Mild fever can actually help the body's **immune system** fight an infection. If a person has a serious illness, he or she may develop a high fever, in which body temperature rises above 105.8°F (41°C). High fever is dangerous, as it can cause **convulsions** and brain damage.

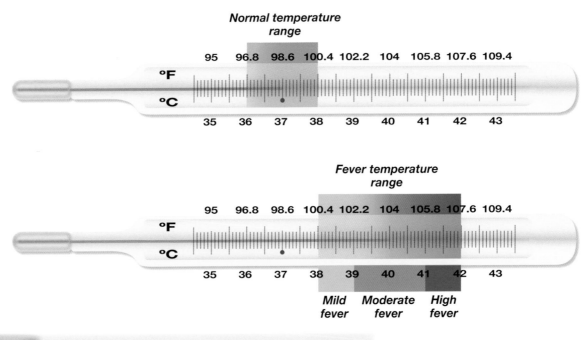

The normal temperature range is 96.8–100.4°F (36.1–37.8°C) (top); the temperature range for fevers can reach up to 107.6°F (42°C) (bottom).

FIRST AID

Treating Fever

People with mild fever should drink plenty of fluids and try to stay cool. Use a wet cloth to bathe the forehead or have a lukewarm shower or bath. People with high fever should be taken to the doctor or to the hospital immediately.

Symptoms of Fever

To find out whether a person has a fever, doctors may look for the signs, or **symptoms**, of fever. People with fevers feel hot and sweaty, start shivering, or have a flushed face. Doctors then check a person's temperature using a thermometer to confirm if the person has a fever.

Diagnosing Illnesses

Fever is often a symptom of another illness, so doctors check for fever to determine what illness a patient has. Fever can be a symptom of both mild and severe illnesses, including colds, pneumonia, tonsillitis, blood poisoning, and malaria. Fever is such an important symptom in some diseases that the disease is named for it. Yellow fever, typhoid fever, dengue fever, and scarlet fever are examples of this.

Parents can check if a child has a fever by using a thermometer.

Did You Know?

Low body temperature is called hypothermia, and it can be just as dangerous as high body temperature. Hypothermia can occur if people are in shock or have been exposed to cold conditions.

GLOSSARY WORDS

immune system a network of systems in the body that fight germs and diseases
convulsions sudden, uncontrollable body movements
symptoms signs that a person may be suffering from a particular disease or illness

Gas is made by the **digestive system**. If gas is trapped, it may make gurgling sounds in the stomach and intestines, or be released as burps or farts.

How Gas is Produced

When people eat and drink, they swallow some air. A series of chemical reactions break down the food so that the body can absorb **nutrients**. These chemical reactions produce gases. When stomach acid passes into the small intestine, a gas called carbon dioxide is produced. **Bacteria** that live in the large intestine produce other gases as they ferment food that is hard to digest.

Belching

Belching, or burping, occurs when gas escapes from the stomach and out of the mouth. The noise is made as gas travels past the **epiglottis** (say epi-GLOT-uhs).

Burps are usually air that has been swallowed. When people are anxious, they may swallow more air than normal, causing them to burp a lot. The air in carbonated beverages can also cause people to burp. Frequent, excessive burping can also be a **symptom** of other stomach problems. Babies get a lot of gas in their stomachs after feeding and are burped by gently patting their backs.

Burps can be caused by the air in carbonated drinks.

? *Did You Know?*

Some people take tablets made of activated charcoal to reduce the smelliness of their flatulence.

Flatulence

Flatulence is the medical name for farting. Flatulence occurs when flatus is released from the intestines and travels out through the anus. Flatus is gas made from swallowed air and other gases, such as hydrogen, carbon dioxide, and methane, which may be produced when the body digests food.

The exact mixture of gases in flatus depends on what people eat and the bacteria that live in their intestines. The gases that make flatus smelly include mercaptans, skatole, and hydrogen sulfide (also known as rotten egg gas). When some foods, such as cauliflower and eggs, are digested, they create large amounts of these gases, producing smelly flatus.

Some foods, such as cauliflower and eggs, are more likely to cause flatulence.

Did You Know?

The average person produces somewhere between 17 and 68 fluid ounces (0.5 and 2 l) of flatus every day.

GLOSSARY WORDS

digestive system	a system of organs and glands that processes food and turns it into energy
nutrients	food or chemicals that the body needs to survive
bacteria	microscopic, single-celled living things
epiglottis	a flap of skin that blocks off the windpipe to stop food entering the lungs
symptom	a sign that a person may be suffering from a particular disease or illness

Growing Pains

Some children get pains in their legs for no obvious reason. These are often called growing pains.

What Are Growing Pains?

Growing pains are aches, usually in the calf muscles, at the back of the knee, and at the front of the thigh. They are often worst in the afternoon, evening, and night. The pain does not go away even if the person changes the position of his or her legs, although it usually disappears in the morning.

About one in five children suffer from growing pains. The pains usually start when a child is between three and five years old, and they can continue until the child becomes a teenager. Growing pains affect equal numbers of boys and girls.

Causes of Growing Pains

No one is sure what causes growing pains. The most likely reasons are tired muscles, caused by lots of physical activity during the day, and poor **posture** that puts strain on certain muscles. Children who are worried or stressed may also suffer from growing pains.

If a child has growing pains, doctors may check his or her legs and knees to make sure that the joints are working properly.

Did You Know?

It was once thought that growing pains were caused by the bones growing, but today doctors know that bones grow very slowly, even during a growth spurt. Some doctors think the name "growing pains" should be changed to "leg aches" because the pain has nothing to do with growing.

Treatment for Growing Pains

There is no medical treatment for growing pains. Sometimes the pain can be reduced with a heat pack and a gentle massage.

For some people, growing pains may be brought on by exercise. However, the pains do not cause any damage to the muscles so it is important to keep exercising in spite of growing pains.

Growing pains may be caused by exercise, as muscles become tired and begin to ache.

HEALTH PROFESSIONALS: Pediatricians

Pediatricians are doctors who are trained to look after the health of children. They diagnose and treat illnesses, and check the health of babies as they grow.

GLOSSARY WORD

posture   the way a person sits or stands

Headaches

Headaches are pains in the head. They are one of the most common illnesses in the world.

Causes of Headaches

There are many causes of headaches. Headaches can occur when the muscles and skin in the back, neck, and head become tightened. They can be caused by increased blood pressure in the brain, inflamed nerves, or infections. Many headaches are the result of referred pain, which means that pain in one area of the body, such as the neck, travels through the nerves to the head. Headaches may also occur when people eat certain foods, do not drink enough water, drink too much alcohol, or stop drinking tea or coffee.

Types of Headaches

Different types of headaches have different causes.

- Tension headaches may occur when a person is worried or stressed. Muscles tighten and blood pressure increases, causing pain in the head.
- Headaches resulting from strain may occur if a person strains his or her eyes by reading in poor light.
- Headaches resulting from illnesses or injuries can occur if a person has an ear or brain infection, or receives a hit on the head.

Headaches can be caused by working on a computer for long periods, which places strain on the eyes.

Did You Know?

The medical term for headache is cephalalgia.

Migraines

A migraine is a type of severe headache in which the **blood vessels** cause the brain to go into **spasm**. People who suffer from migraines have severe pains in their head and may experience other **symptoms** such as vision difficulties, vomiting, and a numb face. More women than men suffer from migraines.

Treating and Avoiding Headaches

Most headaches eventually stop by themselves, but people can treat the pain from a headache as soon as they feel it. People can take drugs, such as aspirin or acetaminophen, to dull the pain. If these drugs do not help, or if a headache continues for more than two days, they should see a doctor.

People can avoid getting headaches by trying not to get stressed, not eating foods that give them headaches, and drinking plenty of water.

People suffering from migraines often have to stay in bed until they recover.

FIRST AID

Treating Headaches
Many headaches occur because people are dehydrated, which means that they have not had enough to drink. Drinking water can be a simple cure for some headaches.

GLOSSARY WORDS

blood vessels	tubes, such as veins or arteries, which blood travels through
spasm	sudden and repeated movements
symptoms	signs that a person may be suffering from a particular disease or illness

Heart

The heart is a muscle that pumps blood around the body.

Healthy Hearts

The healthier a heart, the more blood it can pump in each beat. The heart is a muscle, and it becomes stronger the more it is exercised. Very fit people usually have strong hearts and slow heartbeats. This is because their hearts do not have to pump as often to move their blood into blood vessels. Unfit people have hearts that have to work harder to pump blood into blood vessels.

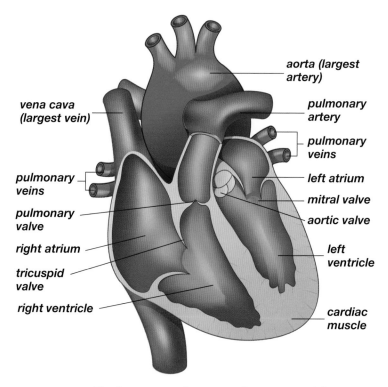

vena cava (largest vein)

pulmonary veins

pulmonary valve

right atrium

tricuspid valve

right ventricle

aorta (largest artery)

pulmonary artery

pulmonary veins

left atrium

mitral valve

aortic valve

left ventricle

cardiac muscle

The heart contains two atria, two ventricles, and several coronary arteries.

How the Heart Works

The heart is divided into four sections, or chambers, called atria and ventricles. There are two atria and two ventricles. Veins drain blood into the atria, which then squeeze this blood into the ventricles. The ventricles then squeeze the blood into arteries, which carry it around the body.

There are **valves** in the heart to stop the blood from flowing backward as it travels through the heart. The heartbeat is the sound of these valves snapping shut after the blood pumps through them.

HEALTH PROFESSIONALS: Cardiologists

Cardiologists (say kah-DEE-ol-UH-gists) are doctors who specialize in treating people with heart problems and operate on hearts. If a heart is very unhealthy, cardiologists can replace arteries and valves. They can even replace a whole heart in an operation called a complete heart transplant.

Detecting Heart Problems

Doctors use stethoscopes to listen to the heart and detect heart problems. They listen for the sound of the valves snapping shut (BOOM boom). Sometimes they hear other whooshing, humming, and rasping sounds. While some people have naturally noisy hearts, unusual sounds can sometimes be a sign that there is something wrong with the heart's structure. These sounds, sometimes called heart murmurs, can indicate that there is a problem, such as a faulty valve or a small hole between the left and right sides of the heart.

Heart Attacks

Heart attacks occur when the flow of blood to the heart is interrupted. The coronary arteries are blood vessels that supply blood to the heart so that it can keep pumping blood. If one or more of these arteries is blocked by a **blood clot** or a fatty buildup, then the heart cannot get enough blood to pump, and it stops. Heart attacks are serious medical emergencies, and sufferers need to be taken to hospital immediately.

artery

artery

If a person's coronary arteries contain large amounts of fat such as this, that person will be at risk of a heart attack.

Did You Know?

The average adult human heart pumps about 5 ¼ quarts (5 liters) of blood every minute.

GLOSSARY WORDS

valves	structures that open to let blood through and close to keep it from returning
blood clot	a clump of semisolid blood

Hiccups

Hiccups are involuntary sounds that are made when the **diaphragm** (say duy-UH-fram) begins to **spasm**.

How Hiccups Form

Hiccups form when the diaphragm spasms and air enters the lungs. When people breathe, they move their diaphragms and the muscles between their ribs. If the diaphragm begins to spasm, the muscles suck air very quickly into the lungs. This makes the **epiglottis** slam shut, causing a "hic" sound.

Causes of Hiccups

No one is sure why the diaphragm begins to spasm. However, certain things are known to trigger hiccups in some people. They include:

- **indigestion**
- eating too quickly
- eating very spicy foods
- drinking alcohol or carbonated drinks
- crying or laughing too much

In rare cases, hiccups might be a **symptom** of another disease, such as pneumonia. They may also occur after a surgery to the chest or abdomen.

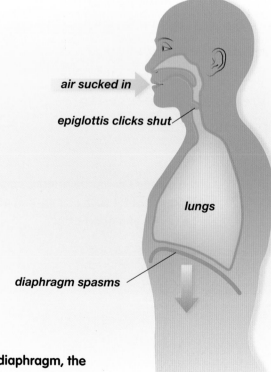

air sucked in

epiglottis clicks shut

lungs

diaphragm spasms

The diaphragm, the epiglottis, and the lungs each play a role in causing hiccups.

? Did You Know?

The medical name for hiccups is singultus.

Home Cures

There are many home cures that people believe will stop hiccups. These include holding their breath, breathing into a paper bag, being given a scare, eating ginger, sitting with their head between their legs, and sucking on a lemon or an ice cube. However, none of these methods has been scientifically proven to cure hiccups. Most cases of hiccups stop after a few minutes, so while it may seem as if the home cure has worked, it is likely that the hiccups would have stopped anyway.

Some people believe that breathing into a paper bag will cure hiccups, because breathing the same air could lead to increased carbon dioxide levels in the blood, which could calm the diaphragm.

Did You Know?

An American man called Charles Osborne had the hiccups for 68 years, from 1922 to 1990.

GLOSSARY WORDS

diaphragm	a large muscle that separates the lungs from the stomach
spasm	sudden and repeated movements
epiglottis	a flap of skin that blocks off the windpipe to stop food entering the lungs
indigestion	difficulty in digesting food, which can cause nausea and stomach pain
symptom	a sign that a person may be suffering from a particular disease or illness

Hormones

Hormones are chemical messengers produced by one part of the body in order to make changes in another part of the body.

Endocrine Glands

Endocrine glands produce hormones and secrete them into the bloodstream. The hormones travel around the body in the bloodstream and help control growth, digestion, and many other body functions. Endocrine glands are found in different parts of the body.

Pituitary Gland

The pituitary gland, which is inside the brain, is very important as it helps to control the hormones made by all the other endocrine glands. If the endocrine glands are damaged and do not produce the right amount of hormones then diseases occur.

Locations of endocrine glands

Gland	Location in the body	Function
Pituitary gland	Inside the **hypothalamus**	Oversees all other hormone levels
Thymus	Inside the chest	Helps to control the level of lymphocytes (white blood cells) in the blood
Thyroid gland	Inside the throat	Controls the **metabolism**
Adrenal glands	On top of each kidney	Make several hormones, including adrenaline
Pancreas	Inside the **abdomen**	Makes the hormone insulin
Ovaries and testes	Ovaries are in a female's pelvis and testes are in a male's scrotum	Make sex hormones

Did You Know?

If a person's diet lacks a trace element called iodine, the thyroid gland in the throat can swell into a lump called a goiter (say goy-TER).

Adrenaline

Adrenaline is a hormone that is produced when a person is faced with a stressful or dangerous situation. If a person sees something that makes him or her anxious, the brain sends a message to the adrenal glands, which make the hormones adrenaline and noradrenaline. These hormones are quickly released into the bloodstream, where they work to increase breathing and heart rate, slow digestion, make the pupils bigger, and contract the muscles. All of these things make a person more alert, faster, and stronger, so that he or she can escape from the danger or confront it.

Puberty

During a period called puberty, changes take place in the body as a child grows into an adult. These changes are controlled by hormones. Puberty starts when the brain sends messages to the ovaries (in females) or the testes (in males). The ovaries or testes then start making different hormones that help a person develop into an adult. Puberty usually begins between the ages of 10 and 12 for girls and between the ages of 11 and 13 for boys.

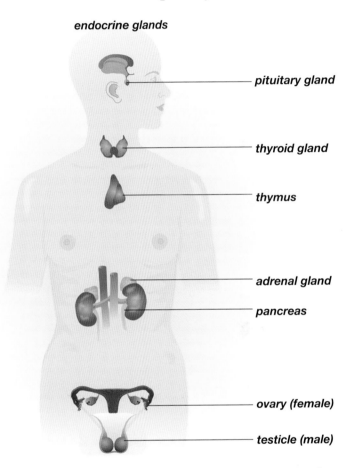

endocrine glands

— pituitary gland

— thyroid gland

— thymus

— adrenal gland

— pancreas

— ovary (female)

— testicle (male)

The endocrine glands are located in different parts of the body, and each produces different hormones.

HEALTH PROFESSIONALS: Endocrinologists

Endocrinologists (say en-DOH-kreh-NOL-oh-GISTS) are doctors who specialize in the treatment of endocrine glands and diseases caused by an imbalance in hormones.

GLOSSARY WORDS

hypothalamus	a part of the brain that monitors hormone levels
metabolism	chemical processes that help the body digest food and turn it into energy
abdomen	a section of the body that includes the stomach, intestines, liver, spleen, and pancreas

Hygiene

Hygiene is another word for cleanliness. It involves doing things in ways that ensure good health.

Washing Hands

Washing hands is an important way to prevent the spread of illnesses, such as colds and **gastroenteritis** (say gas-TROH-en-TUH-ruy-TUS). These illnesses are spread by bacteria, which can get onto the hands when people touch things. Good hygiene involves washing hands after using the toilet, before making and eating food, after handling animals, and after being near someone with a cold.

People should wash their hands before preparing food to prevent the spread of bacteria, which can cause food poisoning.

Food Poisoning

Food poisoning is caused by bacteria living inside food that has been prepared unhygienically. The **symptoms** of food poisoning include stomach pains, **diarrhea**, and vomiting.

To prevent food poisoning, food should always be prepared using clean utensils. Knives and cutting boards should be cleaned after cutting meat so that bacteria cannot **contaminate** other foods, such as salads, that are being prepared. People should not share cutlery when eating, and leftovers should always be stored in an airtight container to prevent contamination by airborne bacteria or flies. Meat and most dairy food should be stored in the refrigerator.

HEALTH PROFESSIONALS: Health Inspectors

Health inspectors usually work for governments. They check that places such as restaurants, hospitals, and public swimming pools are clean and hygienic.

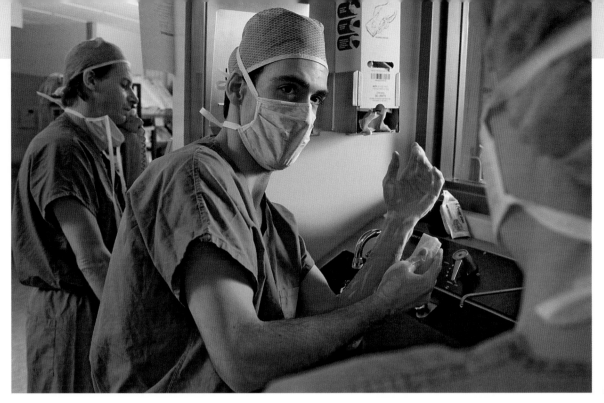

When doctors and nurses wash their hands before surgery, it is known as "scrubbing up."

Medical Hygiene

People working in hospitals have to be very careful about preventing the spread of disease. Doctors and nurses wear special protective clothing during surgery to protect themselves and the patient. Surgeons scrub their arms and hands thoroughly for up to 15 minutes before they put on their gloves to operate on their patients. All medical equipment is either used once or it is **sterilized** carefully before and after each operation. Wounds are covered with bandages and gauze to prevent bacteria from entering.

Louis Pasteur (1822–1895)

Louis Pasteur was a French chemist and microbiologist. He discovered that bacteria and other microscopic organisms caused wine and food to spoil, making the people who ate it sick.

GLOSSARY WORDS

gastroenteritis	an inflammation of the digestive system
symptoms	signs that a person may be suffering from a particular disease or illness
diarrhea	a disorder in the intestines that causes runny feces
contaminate	infect with bacteria
sterilized	cleaned thoroughly to remove all bacteria and germs

Immune System

The immune system helps fight disease and protects the body against **bacteria** and **viruses**.

White Blood Cells

White blood cells are an important part of the immune system. They are made in the bone **marrow**. There are many different kinds of white blood cells, and they work together to protect the body. Neutrophils and macrophages swallow and kill bacteria and viruses that enter the body. B-lymphocytes identify bacteria or viruses and make chemicals called antibodies to fight them. If the particular bacteria or virus has been defeated before, B-lymphocytes will make the same antibodies to kill it again.

The Lymph System

The lymph system helps fight disease by checking for bacteria and viruses in the blood. The system is made up of lymph vessels, which are found throughout the body. Lymph vessels contain liquid called lymph. Lymph is actually **blood plasma**, and it drains from around the cells and organs, eventually mixing back with the blood near the heart. At certain places along the lymph vessels, there are lymph nodes, sometime called glands, which check the lymph for bacteria and remove them.

A doctor may feel the lymph nodes in a person's neck to find out if they are swollen. This is a sign that the immune system is fighting an infection.

Did You Know?

Some diseases are caused when the immune system works in an unexpected way. These include diabetes, rheumatoid arthritis, and many allergies.

This microscopic image shows how white blood cells (shown here in blue) surround and swallow bacteria (shown here in yellow) before they can cause an infection.

Antibodies

Antibodies are a type of chemical produced by the immune system when foreign substances, sometimes called antigens, threaten the body. Each type of antibody defends the body against one specific type of antigen. Antibodies have a special part that is sensitive to a particular antigen and binds to it, making it inactive.

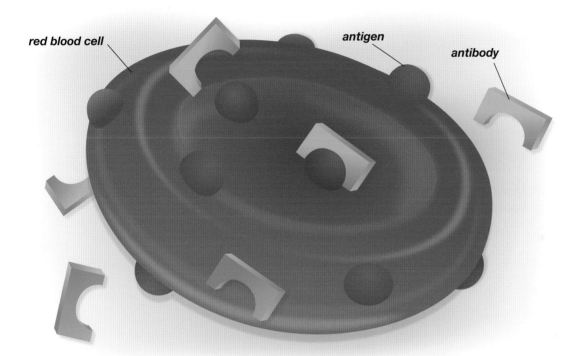

red blood cell

antigen

antibody

Antibodies bind to antigens and disable them.

Keeping the Immune System Healthy

A good diet and plenty of sleep will help keep the immune system healthy. This means that the body will be more prepared to fight illnesses.

GLOSSARY WORDS

bacteria	microscopic, single-celled living things
viruses	microscopic living particles that stop cells from working properly
marrow	a soft, jellylike substance in the center of bones
blood plasma	the liquid part of the blood, without the blood cells

Infections

Infections happen when certain microscopic organisms enter the body and start to multiply.

Causes of Infections

Most infections are caused by bacteria or **viruses**. Bacteria are microscopic, single-celled living things. They are found almost everywhere on Earth, including in the air, soil, water, plants, and animals. Viruses are even smaller than bacteria. They cannot reproduce unless they invade another living thing and use its cells to reproduce. Some infections are also caused by microscopic **fungi** or single-celled animals, such as amebas (say uh-MEE-bahs).

Pus

When bacteria enter the body, the immune system immediately begins working to eliminate them. White blood cells called neutrophils swallow and kill the bacteria. Eventually the neutrophils die.

Pus is a whitish substance made up of dead neutrophils and some bacteria that are still putting up a fight. If a person has a skin infection, the pus can be seen just under the skin. However, the body also makes pus that cannot be seen, such as if a person has **appendicitis** or an ear infection.

A bacterium (magnified here) can cause infectious diseases such as food poisoning.

Earle Dickson (1892–1961)

American Earle Dickson invented Band-Aids® in 1920. He noticed that when his wife cut her fingers while preparing food, the gauze she applied kept falling off her fingers. Band-Aids® help to prevent infections by keeping wounds clean.

Infectious Diseases

Infectious diseases are diseases that spread easily from one person to another. Deadly infectious diseases include Acquired Immune Deficiency Syndrome (AIDS), which is caused by the Human Immunodeficiency Virus (HIV), and malaria, which is caused by a single-celled animal called a plasmodium (say plaz-MOH-dee-UM).

Preventing Infection

There are many ways to help prevent infections, including washing hands after using the toilet and staying away from people who have some types of infectious diseases. If a person is in good health, the body can also fight off many infections by itself.

Wounds must be cleaned carefully and then covered to avoid infection.

Treating Cuts and Scrapes

Cuts and scrapes should be washed with **antiseptic** and then covered so that they do not become infected.

FIRST AID +

GLOSSARY WORDS

viruses	microscopic living particles that stop cells from working properly
fungi	plant-like living organisms
appendicitis	an infection of the appendix, which is a short tube that is attached to the large intestine
antiseptic	a substance that kills bacteria or stops them from growing

Influenza

Influenza is a **contagious** disease caused by a **virus**. It is commonly called the flu.

The Flu Virus

The flu virus is spread from one person to another through coughs and sneezes. Normally, the body will become immune to a virus over time, but the flu virus is able to change itself so that it tricks the immune system. That is why each year people might talk about a new or different **strain** of flu. People may become immune to one strain of the flu, but they will not be immune to future strains.

The Flu and Colds

Many people who have a bad cold often think they have the flu, but they do not. A cold usually lasts for two or three days, but the flu lasts for up to a week. Fever, shivering, and muscle pains are **symptoms** of the flu but not of a cold. People often get runny noses when they develop colds, but this does not usually happen with the flu.

This magnified image shows the Beijing influenza virus (shown in red), which is a very contagious strain of the flu.

FIRST AID

Treating the Flu

The best treatments for the flu are bed rest and drinking plenty of liquids. Antibiotics cannot be used to treat the flu because it is caused by a virus, and antibiotics only treat infections caused by **bacteria**.

Flu Vaccine

In most countries, a flu vaccine is available to protect people against the flu. People must have a new vaccine every year because there are new strains of the flu virus each year. While flu is not usually a serious illness, it can be harmful for people who have weakened immune systems or lungs. Elderly people, asthma sufferers, and people with other illnesses should have annual flu vaccines.

Flu Epidemics

When a new strain of flu virus infects large numbers of people, it is called a flu epidemic. In 1918, there was a serious flu epidemic caused by a severe strain of flu called Spanish flu. It spread to many countries around the world and is estimated to have killed between 20 million and 100 million people.

Many people have flu vaccines each year to protect them from the latest flu strain.

Did You Know?

Some flu viruses can cause illnesses in animals other than humans. A flu virus called H1N1 or swine flu is found in swine. Another flu virus, H5N1 or bird flu is found in birds.

GLOSSARY WORDS

contagious	passes easily from one person to another
virus	microscopic living particles that stop cells from working properly
strain	type of a particular disease
symptoms	signs that a person may be suffering from a particular disease or illness
bacteria	microscopic, single-celled living things

Inherited Diseases

Inherited diseases, or genetic diseases, are passed from parents to children. They are caused by an abnormality in the **genes**.

Genes and Chromosomes

Genes are arranged into chromosomes (say kroh-MUH-sohms), which are found in almost every cell in the body. Chromosomes contain all of the information that makes a person, and each piece of this information is coded by one gene. People inherit two sets of genes, one set from each of their parents. Sometimes genes are faulty or are missing altogether. This can lead to disease.

Different Types of Inheritance

There are different types of inherited diseases. Some, such as Huntington's disease, are caused by one faulty gene from only one parent. People with Huntington's disease usually start to develop brain and nerve damage in their 30s or 40s. Other inherited diseases, such as cystic fibrosis, are caused by inheriting faulty genes from both parents. Children with cystic fibrosis produce large amounts of **mucus** that affects their lungs, liver, pancreas, and intestines.

Did You Know?
Some inherited conditions, such as color blindness, affect more males than females.

Chromosomes (shown in pink) are made up of genes, which carry information that can cause inherited disease.

Carriers

Carriers are people who have only one faulty gene for a disease that needs two faulty genes to develop. If people inherit only one faulty gene, they will not get the disease, but they will carry the gene and could pass it on to their children. Sickle cell anemia is an example of this type of disease. If a person inherits two faulty genes, he or she will develop the disease, in which red blood cells are unusually shaped. However, if the person inherits just one faulty gene he or she will be **resistant** to another disease, malaria.

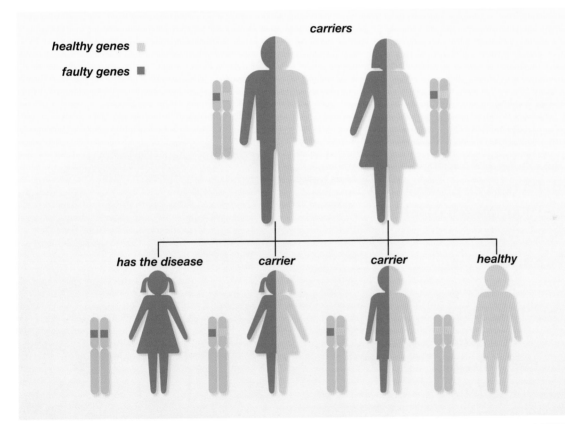

carriers

healthy genes

faulty genes

has the disease   carrier   carrier   healthy

Carriers inherit only one faulty gene for a disease, but they could pass this gene on to their children.

Did You Know?

In the 1800s and early 1900s, members of the royal family of Russia carried an inherited disease called hemophilia. People with hemophilia bleed easily, and their blood does not **clot** properly.

GLOSSARY WORDS

genes	parts of chromosomes that carry codes for particular characteristics
mucus	a thick, slimy body fluid
resistant	immune or less likely to catch a particular illness
clot	dry and form scabs

Itchiness

Itchiness is a sensation on the skin that makes a person want to scratch.

Itch Nerves

Different nerve endings or receptors in the skin are sensitive to heat, cold, pressure, and pain. About one in 20 nerve endings are responsible for itch signals. When something small and light, such as an insect, lands on the skin, the itch nerves are activated. They send signals to the brain to make the body scratch and brush away the insect.

Insect Bites

Insect bites can make some people itch. When an insect such as a mosquito lands on a person, it injects its **saliva** into the skin. The body automatically reacts to the saliva by making **histamine**. Some people have a very strong histamine reaction, and they get a huge bump that itches after a mosquito bite. Other people hardly notice they have been bitten and their bites do not itch at all.

When a mosquito bites, its saliva can trigger a reaction in the body, resulting in an itchy bump.

Did You Know?
The medical name for itchiness is pruritus (say pruh-RUY-tuhs).

Dry Skin and Itching

Skin is constantly repairing and renewing itself from the inside out. Dead skin cells on the surface flake off so that new, healthy ones can move to the surface. People shed dead skin cells when itch signals are sent to the brain, telling them to rub or scratch the skin. Dead skin cells are also shed when skin rubs against clothing and towels.

Itchy Allergies

The body also produces histamine if a person is allergic to a substance that has entered his or her body. Itching is a **symptom** of many allergies, such as hay fever (which causes an itchy nose) and eczema (which causes itchy skin).

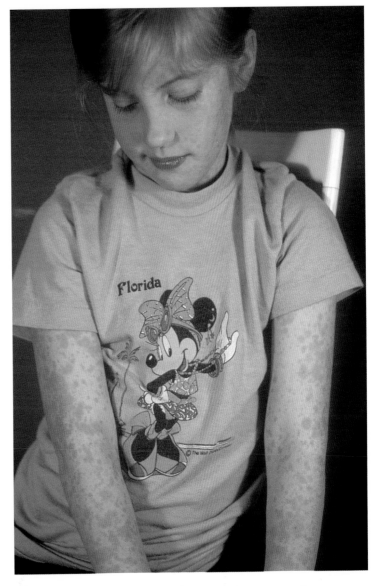

Allergic reactions can cause the skin to become red, dry, and itchy.

Did You Know?

Itching, like yawning, can be contagious. If people talk about itching or watch someone scratching, they can start to get itchy themselves.

GLOSSARY WORDS

saliva	a clear liquid produced in the mouth (also called "spit")
histamine	a chemical released into the bloodstream by white blood cells that helps the body to fight off bacteria and viruses
symptom	a sign that a person may be suffering from a particular disease or illness

Jet Lag

Jet lag occurs when a person's normal daily body rhythms are upset because he or she has traveled in a jet plane across different **time zones**.

How Jet Lag Occurs

Jet lag occurs when people fly across different time zones. For example, the flight from London, England, to Los Angeles takes about 10 hours and crosses several time zones. If a person leaves London at 10 A.M., he or she arrives in Los Angeles 10 hours later, but the local time in Los Angeles will be noon. While the person's body may think it is 8 P.M. and time for bed, the clock says it is only lunchtime.

Symptoms of Jet Lag

People with jet lag can suffer from many different **symptoms** including tiredness, stomach pains, **insomnia**, headaches, **irritability**, and mild depression. These symptoms can last for up to four days. People can get over jet lag more quickly by trying to adjust their sleeping and eating patterns to match those of the place they are in.

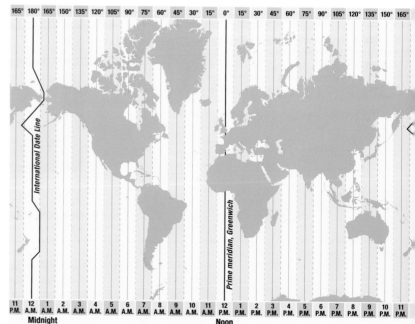

Jet lag occurs when traveling across some of Earth's 24 different time zones.

Did You Know?

Shift workers who sometimes work in the day and sometimes work overnight can suffer from similar symptoms to jet lag.

The Internal Clock

Each day, the body goes through a daily rhythm, which is called the internal clock or the circadian (say ser-KAY-dee-UHN) rhythm. Many of the body's processes, such as hormone production, digestion, heart rate, and blood pressure are timed by the internal clock.

Part of the brain constantly checks the amount of light a person sees. When it begins to get dark, the body produces a hormone called melatonin, which gives the body the signal to fall asleep. If a person changes time zones, the brain will at first continue to make melatonin at the usual time. This means that a person may get tired when it is not time to sleep.

The body produces melatonin at roughly the same time each day, which means that people who are traveling across many time zones could become sleepy in the middle of the day.

Did You Know?

Most people's daily rhythms mean that they are most alert around 10 A.M., their reactions are fastest in the mid-afternoon, and they are strongest in the late afternoon.

GLOSSARY WORDS

time zones	areas on Earth within which the same time is followed, which is often called local time
symptoms	signs that a person may be suffering from a particular disease or illness
insomnia	having difficulty getting to sleep and staying asleep
irritability	grumpiness

Index

Page references in bold indicate that there is a full entry for that topic.